BOOK ANALYSIS

By Tara Dorrell

The Vegetarian
BY HAN KANG

Bright Summaries.com

Shed new light
on your favorite books with

Bright
=Summaries.com

www.brightsummaries.com

HAN KANG 9

THE VEGETARIAN 13

SUMMARY 17

The Vegetarian
Mongolian Mark
Flaming Trees

CHARACTER STUDY 25

Yeong-hye
Mr Cheong
In-hye's husband
In-hye

ANALYSIS 33

The violence of humanity
Points of perspective
Physicality and a vegetative state

FURTHER REFLECTION 41

FURTHER READING 45

HAN KANG

SOUTH KOREAN WRITER

- **Born in Gwangju, South Korea in 1970.**
- **Notable works:**
  - *Greek Lessons* (2011), novel
  - *Human Acts* (2014), novel
  - *The White Book* (2016), novel

Born in Gwangju in 1970, Han Kang is a Korean writer who has published essays, novels, poems and novellas. She comes from a family of writers: her father Han Seung-won is a novelist, and her brother Han Dong Rim is a writer. She studied literature at Yonsei University and first saw her work published in a quarterly called *Literature and Society*. She now teaches creative writing at the Seoul Institute of the Arts and has won the Yi Sang Literary Prize, the Kim Yu-jeong Literary Award and the Man Booker International Prize.

Her work often looks at the consequences of human actions, exploring peoples' motives and both the brutality and empathy humans are capable of. These themes have been examined in her books *Convalescence* (2013) and *Human Acts* (2016), as well as in *The Vegetarian*.

THE VEGETARIAN

A DARK GLIMPSE INTO THE NATURE OF HUMANITY

- **Genre:** novella
- **Reference edition:** Kang, H. (2015) *The Vegetarian*. London: Portobello Books.
- **1st edition:** 2007
- **Themes:** desire, aesthetic beauty, innocence, sanity and insanity, violence, shame, humanity, empathy

The Vegetarian was written in 2015, and was one of Han Kang's first works to be translated into English. It follows a young woman in modern-day South Korea whose decision to give up meat results in destructive consequences for both her and her family. This disturbing but powerful novella explores what it means to be human in a world filled with violence, and the effect human appetite and desire have on those who try to reject them.

Han Kang herself has noted how the book was influenced by the 1980 Gwangju Uprising, a student uprising which was violently put down. The incident has heavily impacted her work and interests, and her preoccupation with humanity, violence and the possibility of innocence is made clear in *The Vegetarian*. The second part of the novella, *Mongolian Mark*, won the Yi Sang Literary Prize in 2005, and was subsequently published as a part of *The Vegetarian*. The English translation of *The Vegetarian* was positively received and won the Man Booker International Prize in 2016.

SUMMARY

THE VEGETARIAN

Han Kang's novella *The Vegetarian* is split into three parts, each one told from a different perspective but always covering the actions or consequences of the decision of one character – Yeong-hye – to stop eating meat. The first part is told from the perspective of Mr Cheong, Yeong-hye's husband. He is a mediocre man with a mediocre life, and describes his wife as being completely average in every way. When he met her, she had fit into his conventional lifestyle perfectly – a docile and dutiful wife who looked after the house and made his meals while earning a minor income. Mr Cheong did not even feel much attraction towards her, believing her sister to be far more beautiful. Nonetheless, this suited him just fine. However, one morning Mr Cheong wakes up to find his wife disposing of all the meat in their house. When he demands answers, she simply tells him that she "had a dream" (p.16). Yeong-hye's dreams depict abstract images of slaughter and bloodshed, and are the cause of both her insomnia and her disgust with any food related to animals. Furious, but unable to stop her, Mr Cheong spends the next several months attempting to both stop her new habits and justify her actions to others. Yeong-hye no longer sleeps, refuses to wear make-up and a bra, and avoids any kind of sexual activity with her husband, who eventually forces her to sleep with him.

After a disastrous work dinner where Yeong-hye refuses to either eat or interact with Mr Cheong's colleagues, he calls his in-laws to inform them of his wife's sudden change in character. Horrified, her family stage an intervention. The entire meal is focused on attempting to convince Yeong-hye to eat, but the situation escalates rapidly when her harsh and hot-tempered father strikes her across the face while Mr Cheong and Yeong-ho, Yeong-hye's brother, hold her down. He then attempts to force-feed her pork, but Yeong-hye retaliates by wrenching away from her family, grabbing a fruit knife and slicing her wrists open. Horrified, her family take her to the hospital, while Mr Cheong realises she is mentally unstable, and has been for some time. Although she recovers, Yeong-hye manages to wander away from the hospital, only to be found by her husband, bared to the waist and holding a bird in her palm, on which there is a "predator's bite" (p. 62).

MONGOLIAN MARK

The second part of the novella is told in the third person by In-hye's unnamed husband, two years after the events of the first part. He works as a video artist, and dreams of filming two people, their bodies painted with vibrant flowers, having sex. Resentful of his wife, whose goodness he finds "oppressive" (p. 72), he instead becomes fixated on his sister-in-law and the purple-blue 'Mongolian mark' on her back. Upon hearing from In-hye that it is shaped like a flower, he obsesses over the idea of painting her naked body and recording her, thus realising his artistic vision. At his wife's request he checks up on the now-divorced Yeong-hye, and is struck by his attraction to her when he finds her alone in her apartment. That night he forces his wife to have sex with him, all the while trying to block out her face.

After persuading Yeong-hye to model for him, he films himself sensuously painting flowers across her body, just as he desired. Deciding the film needs an accompanying piece, he convinces a young friend of his (known only as "J") to be filmed alongside Yeong-hye in a sexually explicit video. He paints the flowers across his friend, but when he asks him to make love to Yeong-hye on camera, J refuses and leaves. Yeong-hye, however, laughingly reveals she has become aroused for the first time in years, claiming it to be because of the flowers, and not his friend. Now desperate for Yeong-hye, In-hye's husband asks a school friend to paint the vivid flowers across his own body. He then returns to Yeong-hye's apartment and records the two of them having intercourse. Upon waking up, he finds his wife in the apartment, having come to check up on her sister. Now believing both her sister and her husband to be mentally unstable, she calls the emergency services. Her husband contemplates committing suicide by jumping off the balcony, but is unable to move and is eventually led away by the authorities.

FLAMING TREES

The final part of the novella is told once more in the third person, this time from the perspective of Yeong-hye's older sister, In-hye. Her husband having left after the incidents of the previous section, In-hye is now the sole carer for Yeong-hye, whose mind and body are rapidly deteriorating. She has been admitted to the Mount Ch'ukseong mental hospital and had initially appeared to be improving, until an incident where she wanders off and is found alone and soaking wet among the trees. In-hye, meanwhile, is struggling to support both her sister and her son as a single mother. Her own depression becomes apparent when she recalls her divorce and questions whether she could have done more to save her sister, both in childhood from their violent father, and as an adult, from Mr Cheong.

By now Yeong-hye has regressed into a near-vegetative state, refusing to eat and instead claiming she is like the trees, needing only water and sunlight to grow. She begins to do handstands to mimic the trees that stand "with both arms in the earth" (p. 153). During one visit to her sister,

In-hye sees the hospital staff force-feed her just as their father had, while threatening to sedate her to prevent her from vomiting the food up. In-hye bites the nurse holding her back from her sister before having her removed from Mount Ch'ukseong. The novella ends with the sisters leaving in an ambulance, watching the trees pass through the window.

CHARACTER STUDY

YEONG-HYE

Although this is a book about Yeong-hye's actions and the consequences they have on both her and her family, it is difficult to call her the protagonist. The closest we come to hearing her own thoughts is through the flashes of her dreams in the first part of the novella, which emphasise the extent to which the dreams take over her life: Yeong-hye becomes overshadowed by the words of her nightmares, which begin to dictate her waking life too. While Yeong-hye's actions are the catalyst for the rest of the book, her significance as a character is dependent on how others perceive and react to her, rather than the ways in which she is allowed to define herself.

Considered "completely unremarkable in every way" (p. 10) by her husband, our first description of Yeong-hye is of an entirely average woman. Of a "middling height; bobbed hair neither long nor short" (*ibid.*), she has no distinguishing features or characteristics. Until her decision to become a vegetarian, the only thing Mr Cheong considers worth noting is her dislike for wearing a bra. In contrast to his indifference to his wife, In-hye's husband finds Yeong-hye far more desirable than her sister, even though he admits the latter is more attractive. To him she "radiates energy" (p. 71), despite her dull clothing and blunt way of speaking. It is worth noting that he compares her to a "tree that grows in the wilderness" (*ibid.*), which coincides with Yeong-hye's own desire to become more plant-like. Yeong-hye's rejection of a human existence results in her bodily physically deteriorating at an alarming rate, and she soon becomes weak and fragile. In In-hye's narrative, she is wasting away, while her mind is now "innocent like that of a child" (p. 133).

MR CHEONG

Husband to Yeong-hye, Mr Cheong narrates the first part of *The Vegetarian*, and it is through him that we see Yeong-hye's decision to stop eating meat and the immediate consequences that follow. Mr Cheong's account is the only one told in the first person, and is unabashedly repugnant, a brutally honest account in which he shows no qualms about his opinions, which he takes to be standard. He has no awareness of how ghastly his thoughts – and later, actions – could be to anyone else; as far as he is concerned, he lives in a patriarchal household in which he is in charge, and Yeong-hye is simply there to comply with his whims. When she starts to deviate from the norms of their marriage, his life spirals out of control and he has no idea how to handle it. Although he believes that he is the one entirely in control in their marriage, as he brings in the majority of their income, he is left at a loss without his wife. Instead, he is now forced to have at least one meal in the house that is entirely vegan, and is utterly unable to stop her. It is likely this inability to stop his wife, who he thought he could control, that agitates him the most.

We get very little physical description of Mr Cheong, only learning from In-hye's artist husband that he has a "dry face" and "vulgar lips" (p. 94). In-hye's husband is far more concerned with Mr Cheong's negative character being in range of Yeong-hye, which according to him would only be "insulting, and defiling, and violent" (*ibid*.). In-hye's own recollections of him give a similarly negative impression of Mr Cheong – finding him to be "cold" (p. 163) when she met him, she "hadn't taken to him at all" (p. 164) and her instinct was to take her sister as far away from him as possible.

IN-HYE'S HUSBAND

In-hye's husband is never named and so is only known through his relationship to his wife. A video artist who rarely produces any work, he is obsessed with Yeong-hye's 'Mongolian Mark' and the idea of filming a video of two bodies, covered with flowers, making love. Like Mr Cheong, he too projects his own ideas onto Yeong-hye, hence his disgust that she could be defiled by someone as "insulting" (p. 94) as her husband. He exploits both her mental state and her body, using the deterioration of her mind to fulfil his desires regarding his work. He also has his own moments of sexual violence, just like Mr Cheong, when his desire for Yeong-hye pushes him to rape her sister, before he forces himself on Yeong-hye too, prior to filming the erotic scene he desired to create. Like her husband, he too places his own agenda on her body, only seeing her for what she represents to him rather than as a person in her own right.

Although he appears to try to be something of a free spirit, his obsession with his work and his sister-in-law result in him neglecting his family. He and In-hye only bother to keep their marriage alive for the sake of their child, when in reality he feels overwhelmed by just how virtuous his wife is, particularly when he desires her sister more.

IN-HYE

In-hye is Yeong-hye's older sister, and is central to the final part of the novella. Considered more beautiful than her sister by Mr Cheong, she is a self-made woman who owns a make-up store and brings in a larger income than her artist husband. Her husband is repeatedly put off by how good a person she is, always feeling "vaguely dissatisfied" (p. 71) with her, despite how thoughtful and kind she is – to him, her "goodness is oppressive" (p. 72). She is without question the most empathetic and caring character in the book, and by the end is looking after both her child and her sister, now as a single mother. Unlike the other narrators, In-hye is also the only one who truly feels regret for how she has used Yeong-hye for her own advantage in the past; much of In-hye's narrative is spent recalling their childhood and wishing she had been less cowardly in the face of their father's wrath.

Despite her independence, the stress of being the sole carer for her sister and son (in addition to being cut off from her parents and fresh out of a divorce) does start to take a severe mental toll on her. She clearly suffers from depression, severe enough to even worry her young child, but regardless of this her main concern is Yeong-hye's welfare. This concern is exacerbated after she sees Yeong-hye force-fed at the hospital, in a manner reminiscent of their father's actions earlier on in the book. During the incident In-hye had been the only one to defend her sister, holding him back "by the waist" (p. 47), as she wishes she had done when he had brutalised them as children.

ANALYSIS

THE VIOLENCE OF HUMANITY

Han Kang uses Yeong-hye's desire to get away from meat and anything related to animals as a metaphor for the desire to escape the violence that humanity can cause. The consumption of meat has always and will always be linked to harming innocent creatures in order to satisfy one's own needs, using animals only for one's own benefit. The destruction humanity can inflict is most easily distinguishable in the men in Yeong-hye's life, all of whom harm her in some way. According to In-hye's narrative, she and her sister grew up fearing their father's aggression, which Yeong-hye was most commonly on the receiving end of. Their father is known for having served in the army during the Vietnam War; for him, brutality was an occupation that he then brought into the home and inflicted upon his children – who, like animals killed for human consumption, are innocent. In-hye had escaped his aggression to some extent by making herself useful as the eldest, and their brother Yeong-ho was left alone because of his gender. Thus, Yeong-hye is the one who was marked as the victim of violence from childhood – and by the end of the novella has been reduced to a child-like state.

Although Yeong-hye might want to separate herself from the killing and harm caused by eating animal products, her decision backfires on her as she is left in the same vulnerable state as any innocent creature, defenceless against the sexual violence of her husband. Just as the meat of animals is eaten and used for humans' own interests, Mr Cheong is likewise only interested in seeking out his own pleasure, with little care or regard for someone else's life. Similarly, In-hye's husband not only uses Yeong-hye to his advantage for the sake of his work, he also forces himself on her before actually filming his final video, overcome by his personal desire for her.

Although like her sister, In-hye also suffers from the violence of men (her husband rapes her too), she is perhaps less of an innocent than Yeong-hye, who she allowed to suffer at the hands of their father to protect herself. As a result, while Yeong-hye (the true innocent) is in an almost vegetative state by the end of the book, her sister is not, even though she too is afflicted by mental illnesses. Han Kang has painted a world in which acts of violence almost ground her characters in reality and allow them to survive. Violence becomes a means to an end for all the characters, a way in which they can further their own interests and benefit themselves – precisely the world Yeong-hye wanted to escape. In-hye's only act of violence as an adult is against the nurse, biting her animalistically. However, it is also the only violent act done with the intention of saving her sister, not for her own benefit and not to harm Yeong-hye as so many others do.

POINTS OF PERSPECTIVE

The first part of the novella is told from the perspective of Yeong-hye's husband: it is through his eyes that we see Yeong-hye's initial rejection of anything related to animals and the changes in behaviour that follow. As we see all these events from the perspective of Mr Cheong, there is a danger of him directing our first impressions of Yeong-hye. Like him, we may at first view her actions as bizarre, incomprehensible and out of the blue, the result of his own inability to comprehend them. However, as Mr Cheong himself is a part of the tale, Han Kang uses his distasteful personality to remind us that this is simply one attitude to Yeong-hye – and not a particularly friendly one at that either. Blunt and honest to the point of making the reader quite uncomfortable, Mr Cheong's repulsion at his wife's vegetarianism is ludicrously excessive, and clearly not the reaction every reader would have. Despite the potential Mr Cheong has to guide our reading of the first part, he is never purposefully manipulative. Repugnant as his character might be, he also genuinely believes everything he says. Han Kang is able to assure us of this through using a first-person perspective for his narrative, which she does not do with any other character. This reaffirms that Mr Cheong truly believes himself to be the victim here – as far as he is concerned, his wife has lost her mind and he is the one who is having to suffer because of it.

Just as Mr Cheong only sees Yeong-hye as his wife, In-hye's husband is also defined by his marriage, as he is never given a name of his own. While this may appear to diminish some of his control, he regains it by using Yeong-hye to his advantage and to fulfil his own dreams, ambitions and desires. He too forces us to see Yeong-hye from his point of view. However, while Mr Cheong wanted a wife who would cater to his every need, In-hye's husband sees in Yeong-hye an ethereal, otherworldly creature whose strange qualities he can fetishize. Although Mr Cheong might have been unabashed in his thoughts, In-hye's husband hides his own desires under the guise of wanting to create art, even when these desires can be just as vulgar as Mr Cheong's – after all, both men still carry out the same violating acts of marital rape.

In-hye provides us with the last perspective, and although she too has used her sister to save herself from their violent father, she is conscious of her actions and feels guilt for them, unlike the two men. Throughout the three parts of the novella the writing style also begins to increasingly switch between tenses. As it progresses it becomes harder to keep track of when and where the narrative is and where it is going. By the time it reaches In-hye's part, we are floating between memories and the present moment – just as Yeong-hye herself no longer seems quite sure of how to exist, In-hye's narrative does not seem to know when it exists. Through the use of different narratives, we can see a progression over the course of the novella from people who will never understand Yeong-hye beyond their preconceived ideas of who she is, to someone who no longer places such judgements upon her and is instead willing to try and understand her for who she is.

PHYSICALITY AND A VEGETATIVE STATE

Over the course of the novella there is a shift in the physicality of the characters from whose perspective the events are recounted. Beginning with the most physically violent narration from Mr Cheong, it then moves on to In-hye's husband and his obsession with the ideas behind his supposedly higher form of art that still uses the most physical of activities. Finally, we come to the character least concerned with physicality, even though Yeong-hye herself has almost entirely deteriorated by this point. In-hye is instead focused on the minds of both herself and her sister. The only central female character provided, she is also the only one to end her part with more understanding of Yeong-hye, beyond the ideas projected onto the woman. Mr Cheong could not comprehend his wife at all, while In-hye's husband only understood her in a physical sense, even when the possibility for a greater connection was there. Throughout the story others have only inflicted harm on Yeong-hye; In-hye is the one to finally take her away from it, actually listening to her sister's wants and pleas.

Yeong-hye herself exhibits a desire to remove herself from the physicality of human life, infused as it is with selfish and harmful actions. Instead, she wishes to subsist as something that does not rely on violence towards other creatures: she discards her clothes as often as she can, "not in the least flustered or embarrassed" (p. 80), thriving when the "sunbeams bathed her" (p. 58), much like a plant. She becomes more alive than she has been in a long time when In-hye's husband paints her with flowers, even to the point of becoming "all wet" (p. 112) for the first time in years. Yeong-hye goes beyond merely becoming a vegetarian – she attempts to become a part of the vegetation, no longer living as another toxic human but simply as an innocent entity whose physical presence can do no harm.

FURTHER REFLECTION

SOME QUESTIONS TO THINK ABOUT...

- Compare In-hye's mental deterioration to Yeong-hye's.
- What is the significance of the violence of the men in the book?
- How does the film adaptation, *Vegetarian* (2010), compare to the novella?
- Explore the marital relations in the book.
- In-hye claims that she felt she "had never really lived in this world" (p. 167). Examine this quote in light of her sister's actions.
- Discuss the significance of Yeong-hye's dreams in the first part of the novella.
- Explore Yeong-hye as a symbol of innocence.
- What is the significance of the title *The Vegetarian*?

We want to hear from you!
Leave a comment on your online library
and share your favourite books on social media!

FURTHER READING

REFERENCE EDITION

- Kang, H. (2015) *The Vegetarian*. London: Portobello Books

REFERENCE STUDIES

- Farrin, C. (2017) Loving the Stranger Beside You: Han Kang's *The Vegetarian*. *Ploughshares at Emerson College*. [Online]. [Accessed 14 February 2019]. Available from: <http://blog.pshares.org/index.php/loving-the-stranger-beside-you-han-kangs-the-vegetarian/>
- Felice, M. (2018) Use of Multiple POV in Han Kang's *The Vegetarian. Failing at Writing and Other Things*. [Online]. [Accessed 14 February 2019]. Available from: <https://failingatwriting.com/2018/08/15/use-of-multiple-pov-in-han-kangs-the-vegetarian/>
- Masad, I. (2016) *The Vegetarian* by Han Kang tells a dangerously defiant love story. *The Guardian, Culture*. [Online]. [Accessed 14 February 2019]. Available from: <https://www.theguardian.com/books/booksblog/2016/dec/23/the-vegetarian-by-han-kang-tells-a-dangerously-defiant-story>

ADAPTATIONS

- *Vegetarian.* (2010) [Film]. Lim Woo-Seong Dir. South Korea: Blue Tree Pictures.

Bright ≡Summaries.com

More guides to rediscover your love of literature

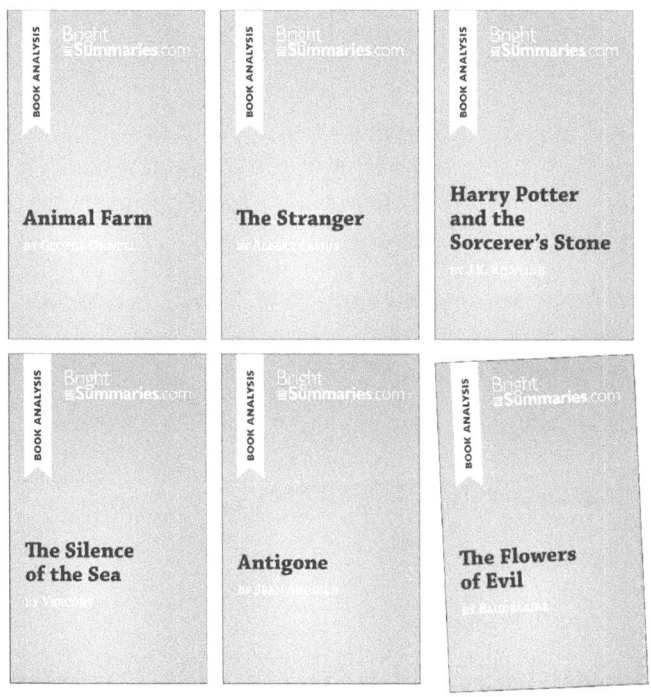

www.brightsummaries.com

Although the editor makes every effort to verify the accuracy of the information published, BrightSummaries.com accepts no responsibility for the content of this book.

© BrightSummaries.com, 2019. All rights reserved.

www.brightsummaries.com

Ebook EAN: 9782808018654

Paperback EAN: 9782808018661

Legal Deposit: D/2019/12603/99

Cover: © Primento

Digital conception by Primento, the digital partner of publishers.

no qualms about his opinions, which he takes to be standard. He has no awareness of how ghastly his thoughts – and later, actions – could be to anyone else; as far as he is concerned, he lives in a patriarchal household in which he is in charge, and Yeong-hye is simply there to comply with his whims. When she starts to deviate from the norms of their marriage, his life spirals out of control and he has no idea how to handle it. Although he believes that he is the one entirely in control in their marriage, as he brings in the majority of their income, he is left at a loss without his wife. Instead, he is now forced to have at least one meal in the house that is entirely vegan, and is utterly unable to stop her. It is likely this inability to stop his wife, who he thought he could control, that agitates him the most.

We get very little physical description of Mr Cheong, only learning from In-hye's artist husband that he has a "dry face" and "vulgar lips" (p. 94). In-hye's husband is far more concerned with Mr Cheong's negative character being in range of Yeong-hye, which according to him would only be "insulting, and defiling, and violent" (*ibid.*). In-hye's own recollections of him give a similarly negative impression of Mr Cheong – finding him to be "cold" (p. 163) when she met him, she "hadn't taken to him at all" (p. 164) and her instinct was to take her sister as far away from him as possible.

IN-HYE'S HUSBAND

In-hye's husband is never named and so is only known through his relationship to his wife. A video artist who rarely produces any work, he is obsessed with Yeong-hye's 'Mongolian Mark' and the idea of filming a video of two bodies, covered with flowers, making love. Like Mr Cheong, he too projects his own ideas onto Yeong-hye, hence his disgust that she could be defiled by someone as "insulting" (p. 94) as her husband. He exploits both her mental state and her body, using the deterioration of her mind to fulfil his desires regarding his work. He also has his own moments of sexual violence, just like Mr Cheong, when his desire for Yeong-hye pushes him to rape her sister, before he forces himself on Yeong-hye too, prior to filming the erotic scene he desired to create. Like her husband, he too places his own agenda on her body, only seeing her for what she